The Divorce Book

Written by Marissa Neira
Illustrated by Francesca Valente

Mommy and Daddy have decided to get divorced. What does that mean? Mommy and daddy will no longer be married, but we are both still your parents. You will gain another home.

Some things will change, but we will always be a family. We will always love you. You will never have to choose between us. Mommy and Daddy are still a team when it comes to parenting you, which means we are all on the same side.

You will spend some of your time with Daddy and some of your time with Mommy. You will have more 1 on 1 time with each of us than you're used to.

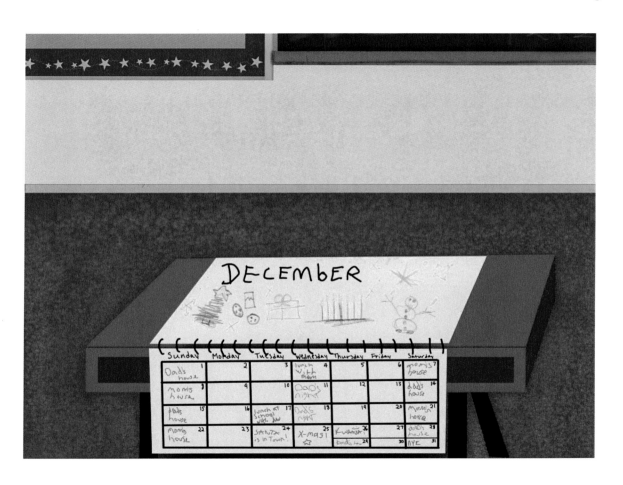

You will have a home with Mommy and a separate home with Daddy. You get to live in two homes! We will do everything we can to help you feel comfortable.

It's okay to ask questions. It's okay to have feelings about this big change. We are both here for you and you can talk to us about anything. None of this changes how much we love you.

If there is something we can do to help you adjust, don't be afraid to ask. We want to make this as easy as possible for you. Remember that you are NOT the reason we decided to get a divorce.

Daddy and Mommy decided to get a divorce because we agreed that we would be happier if we weren't married. When your Mom and Dad are happy, it makes us better parents. You are our top priority, and we are committed to being the best parents we can be for you. You mean the world to us!

Divorce doesn't change our love for you. We love you very much. Divorce does change our family dynamic. We may have separate houses and separate celebrations. Just think of it as double the fun.

This will get easier over time. Many kids have divorced parents. You are not alone!

Mom and Dad are not going to be married anymore, but we are still a team! We are here to help you and we want you to know that everything will be okay. You have two parents who love and support you. That will never change.

The End...

Just means a new beginning.

Made in the USA
Las Vegas, NV
28 April 2024